Oppressionless

George Bloomer

Unless otherwise indicated, all Scripture quotations are taken from the *New King James Version* of the Bible.

Printed in the United States of America

ISBN 1-892352-01-X

George Bloomer
P.O. Box 11563
Durham NC 27703

Dedication

This book is dedicated to the Bethel Family Worship Center church family—elders, ministers, and entire staff. Also to Kimberly Meadows for all the transcription and for making the manuscript possible.

Acknowledgment

I would like to acknowledge my pastor of eight years, Bishop Roderick R. Caesar Jr., and the Bethel Gospel Tabernacle Church family for their support and love and for the role they played in helping my spiritual life to mature.

Contents

Foreword

No one doubts the enormous threat to society brought on by *oppression* in all its forms. Governments use oppression in many nations to control and hold captive their citizens. Some husbands and wives try to "get their way" by using mental, verbal, or physical forms of oppression on each other or their children.

Oppression is not merely the emotional effect felt when someone has a bad day. It is a spiritual attack, usually brought on by Satan against people that Jesus died for!

In this brilliant book, *Oppressionless*, Pastor George Bloomer begins to unmask the very root causes of oppression, depression, and recession, which usually begin in early childhood. His humble beginnings in life and his rapidly increasing stature today as a father, husband, pastor, and author uniquely qualifies him to speak into your life on this topic. The Holy Spirit has led him in writing this book, and in it I believe you will find solutions—not just pat answers—to one of mankind's greatest dilemmas. Since oppression is such a great problem in our society today, doesn't it stand to reason that *God* would address it proportionally in His Word?

I pray that as you read these pages, the anointing of the Holy Spirit will wash away years of hurt, discouragement, and confusion. You are going to laugh and cry when you see yourself in the pages of this book. Then you are going to shout for joy when you realize how you can be released from yesterday and tomorrow's fears!

Buckle up your seat belt and get ready for the drama of deliverance as God speaks to you personally and also prepares you to help set someone else free from oppression. You can only rise in life to the level of your knowledge. Pastor Bloomer's excellent insight can help you break the bands that have hurt you and held you back for so long. Get ready to learn a new song for yourself—"FREE AT LAST!" That is what will happen as you read this book.

In honor of my friend and true brother in Christ,

Walter Hallam

Introduction

Growing up under the welfare system, I witnessed first hand the dependency that develops from relying on government assistance and the oppression that consumes America's welfare state. As I grew from adolescence into adulthood, the bondage of oppression took me to prison, where I met the only One Who has the power to set the oppressed free.

As I will disclose in the following pages, oppression is a satanic spirit. It is a demon assigned by Satan that will attempt to trap a victim through a series of circumstances. Poverty is just one of his most visible circumstances. If Satan can get his victim oppressed, he will send a spirit of depression to disconnect its victim from any influence but him. And he will attempt to do this with Christians as well as the unsaved.

The oppressed adult is often frustrated, overly sensitive, and jealous. Does any of this sound familiar to you? If it does, it is my hope that this book will give you the knowledge, faith, and courage to help others, and even yourself if you need to be free. Oppressionless living is possible, as are all things, to those who truly believe that Jesus is the One who sets the captive free (Mark 9:23).

George Bloomer

"And you shall know the truth,
and the truth shall make you free."

–John 8:32

1

OPPRESSION

Social Menace: Demonic Foe

Growing up under the welfare system, I witnessed first hand the dependency that develops from relying solely on government assistance to feed a family and manage a household. This same dependency spilled over into my adulthood as I began to feel that people should automatically give to me, and accommodate me whenever I needed help.

The power of God eventually broke this way of thinking as I learned that man should not live by bread alone, but by every word that comes from the mouth of God (see Matthew 4:3). When we look to God, He will show us how to take care of ourselves.

Life as I know it today is void of any dependency on men. Instead, I depend totally upon God for my livelihood and my well-being. But this isn't the case for millions of people—including more than we would want to admit who are born-again members of Christ's church.

Our prayer within my family during our hard times and seasons of oppression was, "Lord, give us this day our daily bread" (see Matthew 6:11). And as we applied faith with this prayer, the dependency and oppressive spirit that had been hovering over us eventually began to lift. Yes, we were taken care of, but we were oppressed. We were downtrodden and miserable until Jesus gave us a lift.

Identifying the Thief

Generally speaking, *oppression* can be defined as "a heavy, weary feeling of the body or mind." Spiritually speaking, oppression is a demonic spirit. When one is feeling the "crunch" of life, fear can set in as a masquerading defense, setting the individual up for a total shutdown. Those who succumb to this emotional ploy are totally unaware of fear's masquerade, and they are further lured into the deceptive clutches of Satan.

As you will discover in the following pages, oppression comes in many different forms and can enter a person's life through a variety of avenues. But one thing is consistent: Anytime the spirit of oppression is in operation, there is a universally acknowledged heaviness that attaches itself to the physical and spiritual being of the one being oppressed. This spirit will also present a struggle between the will of God and the will of man, and will try to pull one down, ultimately to death.

Anyone who has received Christ as Lord in his life and is loving God wholeheartedly, yet still can't let go of that *one thing* that holds him captive to sin, is struggling with the spirit of oppression. As his born-again human spirit and his fallen sinful flesh engage in battle, the body becomes fatigued and sluggish, causing further bewilderment within the mind. At this stage of the battle, the believer must make a decision to either buffet the flesh and surrender to the will of

God or become so perplexed by Satan's lies that he gives up.

Unfortunately, many times the oppressed Christian decides within himself that he can no longer go on under the heaviness of the oppression that he is forced to endure. So it seems easier and less of a burden to just give up. Rather than to continue fighting what the enemy has convinced him is "a losing battle," he gives up and gives in to the sinful drives of the flesh.

Oppression can originate in early childhood and can become a major factor in the shaping of a child's identity. If a child is constantly discouraged, belittled, embarrassed, and humiliated by words of discouragement, his life can be framed within these barriers. The child then grows up to be an adult with low self-esteem and emotional dependencies. He struggles to succeed, but the lingering spirit of oppression controls his life and keeps him down.

Frustrated, overly sensitive, jealous, and competitive, the oppressed adult is incapable of handling constructive criticism. He reaches after his goals and ambitions as he trudges through one disappointment after another. Unable to face the risk of another letdown, he gives up again and again. Instead of allowing God to steer his life in the right direction, life controls him and weighs him down as a heavy burden.

This isn't a pretty picture. But the sad fact of the matter is you probably know someone like this. You may even *be* someone like this yourself.

Depression—Oppression's Killing Partner

Depression is one of the major side effects of the spirit of oppression. Depression will make one gloomy and cause what many call "low spirits." This condition destroys the mind, clouds the thinking, and further oppresses the individual who is already consumed by his burdensome state.

Six Warning Signs

Like oppression, depression is no respecter of persons. It crosses gender, race, and every social line and class. According to the *American Psychological Association*, some of the warning signs of depression are:

- Sleep disturbances—inability to sleep, sleeping too much, or irregular sleep patterns.
- Appetite disturbance—eating far more or less than usual.
- Social withdrawal—refusal to go out.
- Blaming yourself for your problems—feelings of worthlessness.
- Inability to concentrate—even on routine tasks.
- Substance abuse—alcohol or drugs.

Every one of these warnings indicates a tearing down of the body and mind. The enemy knows that if he can afflict the body through robbing it of food and sleep, in a matter of time, the body will collapse.

But even more dangerous than these physical signs are Satan's devious, subtle ways of initially severing all contact and communication with loved ones and friends. Within this oppressing strategy lies his ability to secretly creep into the door as your only means of communication. It is here where he deceives and disrupts the mind, eliminating those who care for you so he may have free rule and reign. Satan then becomes the authoritative figure in his victim's life. I believe this may be why many times women seem to be more susceptible to the spirit of depression than men.

Women are by nature communicators. So when a woman's communication is cut off from friends and loved ones, the enemy immediately makes it his business to inhabit that newfound void in her life. And he does it through corrupt communication. This devious form of communication can be mentally implanted through subconscious thinking or ungodly counsel.

This is why I believe women who aren't engaged in some sort of social or religious activities outside of the home can be more susceptible to oppression. It has been found that women who have structured themselves in multiple roles experience less depression than those who focus their lives in one area.

For instance, a single mother of three who is trapped within the welfare system and sits home all day watching soap operas and talk shows becomes major prey for the spirit of oppression. The enemy speaks to her mind through his fallen TV shows, causing her to give up and become depressed. Perhaps this is because the welfare system itself is a curse and carries with it a spirit of depression.

Think about it: its name and all it stands for came from the greatest depression of them all—the great depression of the 1930s. So although the word *welfare* means "the state of well-being and prosperity," it still has not survived the curse attached to its name because of the false sense of security brought on by the welfare system. It has been said that one of the reasons the great depression bankrupted America was because the wealth at that time had been unequally distributed. And that caused the stock market to become highly exaggerated, only to eventually crash, leaving the economy in a disaster. October 29, 1929 marked not only a great decline in the economy but in the hope and self-esteem of American society, as people were forced off their jobs with no means of support for their families. This day was known as "Black Tuesday."

Herbert Hoover was president at that time, and although he tried to keep hope in the hearts of the poor, people realized his words were empty, with no proof to back them up. Franklin Delano Roosevelt defeated Hoover soundly at the polls at the close of Hoover's first term. Roosevelt's "New Deal" government work programs were then quickly implemented to help America out of those bleak days.

Years later, President Lyndon Johnson appeared on the scene, declaring "War on Poverty" with such programs as welfare AFDC (Aid to Families with Dependent Children), food stamps, and Medicaid. But without the proper structure and supervision, these same programs proved to be a curse to many families. Some families have gone through generations depending solely on welfare as a means of support.

I say this not only because I personally grew up under the welfare system, but because there are numerous children who are actually birthed into oppression through welfare and government. They, particularly, are among the many who grow up to become adults with the oppressive behaviors and dependencies previously mentioned. The curse of low self-esteem and the spirit of criticism is oppressing millions within the welfare system.

Without a relationship with God or divine intervention, the welfare dependent's desire to better himself eventually dies. He finally gives up because flesh warring against flesh and flesh warring against the Spirit will eventually wear out the body and tear down one's mind.

Welfare and the dependency that accompanies it is committed to making one a part of a permanent underclass. Because it is a curse, the system of welfare not only affects people financially, it affects them emotionally as well. It is very degrading.

Yet the illusion says, "Don't be embarrassed—hold your head up. You deserve this. And besides, if you don't get it, someone else will." The enemy then continues the lies by telling you that you can't get a job because no one is hiring, furthering the length of your impoverishment.

Welfare also separates the family, putting asunder the greatest institution on earth—marriage. The Bible says, *"Therefore what God has joined together, let not man separate"* (Matthew 19:6). But welfare says if there is a man (a husband) in the home—you can't receive assistance. This rule encourages "shacking up" and lying to stay afloat. God says marriage is honorable in the sight of the Lord, yet in the welfare system, marriage is discouraged and penalized without warning. This unreasonable policy makes no room for an individual to gradually be weaned from the system to avoid economic ruin. The weapons of God's warfare are needed in this devilish fight.

> *For the weapons of our warfare are not carnal but mighty in God for pulling down strongholds* (Ephesians 6:18).

So, even though welfare has proven to be helpful, this is normally the exception instead of the rule. Many people take what was meant to be a temporary means of support and turn it into a lifetime of simple survival. As a result, the spirit of oppression is left hovering over generations of children who grow up lacking any initiative or drive to do better.

No matter how long an individual has been held captive by the spirit of oppression, he or she is never too young or old to be set free. One touch from God can loose a multitude of curses. The Word of God teaches that whatever you bind on earth has already been bound in heaven, and whatever you loose on earth has already been loosed in heaven (see Matthew 16:19).

The Word of God sets men free when it is received as food for life and vision.

> *Blessed is the man Who walks not in the counsel of the ungodly, nor stands in the path of sinners, nor sits in the seat of the scornful; but his delight is in the law of the Lord, and in His law he meditates day and night* (Psalm 1:1,2).

In the chapters that follow, I will attempt not only to enlighten, but to break this vicious cycle of oppression, so that you will have God's power for oppressionless living. But remember, God's delivering power must be received with responsible faith. He offers no government freebies. His hand is always out, but we must reach up—not out.

2

MY TRIBUTE

Free at Last

Happy is he who has the God of Jacob for his help, whose hope is in the Lord his God, Who made heaven and earth, the sea, and all that is in them; Who keeps truth forever, Who executes justice for the oppressed, Who gives food to the hungry. The Lord gives freedom to the prisoners (Psalm 146:5-7).

Oppression knows no boundaries. It permeates the welfare state that I grew up under, producing thousands of hopeless lives. But it also stalks the business and educational communities, because misery and failure know no social boundaries. And, yes, it stalks the church in an effort to cripple born-again believers with heaviness and fear.

Wherever this spirit can find a foothold, it will work to confuse, distract, and cut off its victim from outside contact. Then it will fill that void with more deception to control clear-thinking minds. Sow an unchecked oppressive thought—and it will reap depression. And once depression sets in, it will reap a harvest of sinful defeat.

Growing up in the church, I found out how one can presume to be free while at the same time falling prey to the tormenting spirit of oppression. It happens without people even realizing what is taking place. This spirit isn't always as overt in a person's life as one may tend to think. In many instances, certain emotions can be so suppressed that the person being oppressed may never realize the reality of their state. Childhood or adult traumatic experiences are sometimes responsible for oppression's delusion.

There are some instances, however, in which an oppressed individual is very knowledgeable of their state, but they can't imagine "how" God could ever set them free from such a powerful stronghold that has been part of life for so many years. Nevertheless, God knows exactly what area to touch...and at what particular time to bring forth deliverance.

When I was eleven years old, I finally got up enough boldness to talk to a young girl who was at that time "the girl of my dreams." Though young in age, I had grown to love this girl with all my heart. Talking to her made everything else seem unimportant. But her mother viewed me as a nobody.

"I don't want to ever see you talking to my daughter again!" she once told me. "A 'Bloomer' will NEVER have a relationship with or be seen with a member of the Thomas family. So stay away from my daughter.

"You're no good and you'll never amount to anything.

"Nothing good could ever come out of your family!

"Your brother is a drug addict, your mother is an alcoholic, and your daddy is no good!" she screamed.

There I stood, an eleven-year-old boy in a nothingless body of mixed emotions. My heart felt as if it had been torn out, and any self-esteem I may have had suddenly exited my entire being. I was oppressed.

As time passed, I was able to put this incident behind me and erase it from my past. Or so I thought. But a number of other experiences would continue to play out within my childhood that would soon spill over into my adult life, forming me because of my past.

The A-Word

One of those oppression-forming experiences was sexual **A**-buse. It happened when I was twelve. At a time when I was totally oblivious to the full nature of sexuality, a woman of experience took it upon herself to teach me about sex and sexuality. For two long years, I was repeatedly called upon by this woman to indulge in sexual acts that a boy my age shouldn't have known about. To her it meant nothing—but it later caused me some temporary problems.

I bring this up to say I'm convinced that because of the oppression I endured from this woman, the door was opened later in my life to more perversion, whoredom, and lawlessness. These were all oppressive spirits that came to strip me not only of my dignity, but to destroy my character. I had convinced myself that time had healed me of these incidences. But I eventually found out that they had only been suppressed, and that the spirit of oppression had packaged them neatly only to open them later as a means of escape.

By the time I was a teenager, I'd already been introduced to drugs, and I had developed a $270-per-day cocaine habit. To support this habit, I did whatever I was "bold" enough to do—snatching purses, robbing, stealing—all to satisfy my habit and to hide within my secret place of escape. It eventually took a sentence in Rikers Island Prison for God to finally get my attention. But true deliverance from my other childhood traumas wouldn't take place until years later. And it came at an unexpected place and an unexpected time.

After having preached all over the country, some fourteen years later I decided to return to the place of my childhood, the Redhook Projects. I preached there three nights amid hundreds who came out to see me. Here I was, one who had escaped the trap of project living, and I was now proclaiming the life of Christ.

Then on the final night, I was approached by an older woman as the meeting concluded. She said hello, so I returned her greeting—but I had no idea who this lady was. She greeted me again, but introduced herself this time as the mother who had forbidden my relationship with her daughter when I was eleven years old.

"Hi," she repeated, "it's me, Ms. Thomas, Tara's mother." Immediately upon recognizing her, I was subconsciously thrust back into my eleven-year-old body. My memory drifted back, and I saw this woman in her younger years, screaming and demeaning me in front of her daughter. Because my heart of stone had been turned to flesh through Christ's conversion, I was able to withhold my emotions and indulge in conversation with her. The hard-core lifestyle Ms. Thomas had endured within the projects showed on her face. She reeked of cigarette smoke, and her wrinkled countenance reminded me of how much time had passed. As I snapped back to the present, I asked, "How is Tara?"

"Well, George," she answered, "Tara isn't doing too well. She has AIDS, and she has five babies—two of which are crack babies, and two others who were born with AIDS." Too stunned to even say anything more, I stood gazing at this woman as she turned and walked away. As she started to walk out of my presence, suddenly she stopped and said, "I sure do wish things could have worked out between you and Tara."

At that moment, the oppressive weight of this woman's words that had been tied around my neck—which I hadn't known was present and had subconsciously suppressed—finally dropped off of me. For fourteen years I had been carrying the weight of this woman's pronouncement that I would never amount to anything. And subconsciously it had caused me to feel less than capable of fulfilling the call of God upon my life. Then, in an instant, God used this same woman to speak words that to some might seem irrelevant—but they set me free of an oppression that I had no idea was hovering over my life.

Until that incident, my insecurities had led me constantly to seek the approval of others. But suddenly the little boy in me symbolically caught up with my manly body. The little hands and arms that had secretly been dangling inside my grown-up body grew into the man's hands and arms, and the little legs and feet stretched forth to finally merge with the man's legs and feet. With everything in proper proportion and working in the right sequence, I was then able to walk like a complete man.

Deliverance, in its most quiet yet powerful form, had taken place. As I stood there in amazement, fighting back the tears that suddenly began to flow down my cheeks, I felt cleansed from the spirit of oppression.

Today I no longer seek unreasonable approval of others. I am free to allow God to speak instead. Then, without questioning my own abilities, I obey. For now I know that it is not me who does the work but Christ who lives within me. I can now walk free of the spirit of inferiority and low self-esteem. I freely preach, proclaiming that God is indeed real and that He will perform His Word until the end. The little boy in me who I knew at that time is now nonexistent. God knew what area to touch at what particular time, in order to bring forth deliverance in my life.

Yes, I had been saved and cleansed by Jesus' blood. And for years I grew and flourished in His grace and the call on my life. But there was a hidden enemy within my mind that had been suppressed, and it was still very active in my decision-making processes. It makes me wonder how many Christians today still have that little boy or girl inside of them, steering them away from God's best? If this is you, I invite you to repeat this prayer:

Father God, in Jesus' name, I come to You and ask for cleansing from _____________. I am a new creature in Christ, but I have never asked for freedom from this particular problem. So I'm asking You now. I lay this situation on the altar, Jesus, and ask You to set me free. In Jesus' name I pray. Amen.

> *"For every one who asks receives, and he who seeks finds, and to him who knocks it will be opened"* (Matthew 7:8).

3

OPPRESSION, DEPRESSION, AND POSSESSION

Satan's Demonic Trio of Progressive Insanity

Obviously, I shared only part of my overall oppression deliverance experience in Chapter 2. By the time the weight of this lingering burden was released through my encounter with Ms. Thomas, I had been cleansed by the blood of Jesus and empowered by His Spirit. And I had been through many other cleansing processes, as are all Christians as they grow in faith. But Satan had a foothold, and I finally broke his hold.

The Word of God presents the nature of Satan like no other document. We can see his history, his driving motivations, and his ultimate destination—hell. In the meantime, he means to oppress and destroy as many lives as possible. So to effectively defeat the spirit of oppression, we must be wise, swift, and alert to the tactics of Satan's devices.

One of Satan's best weapons is to send natural occurrences to frustrate you spiritually. He will do this continually if he can. And unless you become skilled in recognizing his tactics, you will spend time in constant, tiresome battles, warring with the natural mind. And because of it, you'll always feel bogged down and depressed.

It is in the midst of these natural occurrences that the door is opened to the spirit of oppression. When it enters to rest upon a person, it causes a weight that can ultimately suffocate the life out of that individual while he or she is ignorant of the origin of the initial attack.

This is why 2 Corinthians 10:3,4 says:

> *For though we walk in the flesh, we do not war according to the flesh: For the weapons of our warfare are not carnal but mighty in God for pulling down strongholds.*

And this is why Proverbs 4:23 admonishes us: *Keep* [guard] *your heart with all diligence.* It is important to guard our hearts so that even when Satan's attacks surface and the mind has been clouded by frustration, he still can't reach the spirit. If man's spirit can be oppressed, destruction not only is knocking at the door, it is destined to take place—that is, unless the individual becomes wise and invokes God's power to finally be set free.

First Samuel 18:10-12 tells us that King Saul was oppressed by an evil spirit. But the power of God through the music of David overwhelmed the spirit, saving David's life.

> *And it happened on the next day that the distressing spirit from God came upon Saul, and he prophesied inside the house. So David played music with his hand, as at other times; but there was a spear in Saul's hand. And Saul cast the spear; for he said, "I will pin David to the wall with it." But David escaped his pres-*

ence twice. Now Saul was afraid of David, because the Lord was with him, but had departed from Saul (1 Samuel 18:10-12).

Oppression Is a Weight

Oppression is like a weight, and Hebrews 12:1 says, *...let us lay aside every weight, and the sin which so easily ensnares us, and let us run with endurance the race that is set before us.* In so doing, we stay free from the enemy's trap.

Oppression carries with it a spirit of illusion that clouds the mind and confuses the thinking, causing one to stray and wander without direction and purpose. It is while a person is in this state that Satan lunges for the kill. And his victim doesn't even realize what is hitting him.

Such was the case of a young woman who shared with me how, out of nowhere, she went from living a very comfortable lifestyle to suddenly losing everything she had. In her own words, she stated, "I closed my eyes for a second and my entire world changed, forcing me to ask myself, 'What happened?'

"One day," she continued, "I had two cars, money, a house, and I wasn't really wanting for much of anything. Then in an instant, I opened my eyes and had nothing."

Without warning, this woman found herself in debt, with nowhere to turn, wandering in a state of confusion. Life had become an illusion, and she didn't know right from left.

Beep! Beep!

Do you remember in the old Warner Brothers Road Runner cartoons how the Coyote would paint a picture of a tunnel against a brick wall in an attempt to stop his competitor? And how the Road Runner would "Beep Beep" and run straight through the tunnel? Then the Coyote—the one who had painted the illusion—would attempt to run into the tunnel after that sneaky bird, but he would smash into his own illusion, sending birdies flying everywhere.

Wiley Coyote and the Road Runner always gave me a good Saturday morning laugh—but this was a only cartoon, where anything can happen. But in real life, the illusions presented by Satan will smash its intended victims straight into the rocks. If you have been aimlessly smashing into brick walls, be encouraged—there is hope. After smashing into phony tunnels for years, when the spirit of oppression lifts, so does the spirit of illusion. However, those who find freedom sometimes find themselves aged beyond their years because they have wasted so much time in a world that doesn't really exist. But the important thing is that they find freedom. Those who never find deliverance just keep on smashing away until death.

Oppression's Partner—Depression

Oppression is accompanied by a subliminal voice that subtly implies its intentions. It comes to demolish the spiritual house that God has built. In its initial stages, it is not a possessing demon, yet it gives a prelude to the inevitable. It is in this stage that the demon paints a picture and sells it to you, while keeping you ignorant of the fact that you are actually being oppressed.

Many times it takes total destruction before one even realizes that he is in a state of oppression. It is then, in the midst of destruction, that oppression calls on depression, whispering deviously, "I've destroyed the house. Now you come in and make him worry about it!"

So depression and oppression join forces to finally collapse their victim's world. Partnering together they attempt to alienate and suffocate their prey, while at the same time whispering in their ears, "Now you can do nothing but worry about your impossible predicament."

And again, it all starts with natural occurrences, which Satan uses to frustrate and oppress people spiritually. If you're the one under attack, suddenly you'll find yourself held hostage to past mistakes. You'll start questioning and badgering yourself over things that have long since passed.

Finally, you'll be deceived into thinking there are no real solutions to the problem. So you'll weep and give up, sometimes even going into a rage as you fall deeper and deeper into a destructive point of no return.

Depression is looked upon as a mental illness and a chemical imbalance that is oftentimes treated and suppressed with prescribed medications. We as Christians, however, know that it is a demon. Medication doesn't provide deliverance. In many cases, it even produces adverse effects. Instead of uplifting the afflicted individual, it can cause confusion and suicidal tendencies.

Depression brings the spirit of fear, doubt, and unbelief. It causes a person to worry about things he can't change, and makes him doubt that God can bring deliverance. Generally this person fears everything. Depression tries to convince its recipient that no one cares, and finally poses the question, "Why don't you just kill yourself?"

It is at this critical point that one **must** hear from God. Depression has been allowed to run rampant in many churches because some pastors pamper the demon instead of walking in the authority to cast it out.

Elizabeth and Mary

One area that often opens the door to depression is low self-esteem. One apparent case of depression that ended in victory is the story of Elizabeth. She and her cousin Mary had many similarities: neither had borne a child, both eventually carried sons and were given the son's names in advance. Both sons were sent by God for the purpose of salvation.

Luke 1:24,25 sets the stage:

> *Now after those days...Elizabeth conceived; and she hid herself five months, saying, "Thus the Lord has dealt with me, in the days when He looked on me, to take away my reproach among men."*

In Luke 1:26-35, we find that an angel spoke to Mary about conceiving and giving birth to Jesus. Then he gave Mary further insight:

> *"Now indeed, Elizabeth your relative has also conceived a son in her old age; and this is now the sixth month for her who was called barren. For with God nothing will be impossible." Then Mary said, "Behold the maidservant of the Lord! Let it be to me according to your word." And the angel departed from her. Now*

> *Mary arose in those days and went into the hill country with haste, to a city of Judah, and entered the house of Zacharias and greeted Elizabeth. And it happened, when Elizabeth heard the greeting of Mary, that the babe leaped in her womb; and Elizabeth was filled with the Holy Spirit. Then she spoke out with a loud voice and said, "Blessed are you among women, and blessed is the fruit of your womb!"* (verses 36-42).

We often misunderstand verse 41, which says it was Elizabeth who was filled with the Holy Ghost, not John. This is very important because before Elizabeth was saluted by Mary, Elizabeth may have been in a state of depression over her barren womb, so she needed the power of God to ward off the spirit of oppression and depression in her life.

But God fulfilled His plan, and the story had a happy ending.

Oppression Leads to Possession

Unless the power of God becomes present in an individual's life, depression will ultimately connect with the demon of possession to build strongholds that could take years to overcome. There is a systematic progression. What begins through natural events, introducing an oppressing force in a person's life, is further frustrated by a spirit of depression. Then when depression is ready, it will call in a spirit of possession (if the victim blindly accepts it)—to finally wipe out his life.

Oppressive spirits are *squatters*—they have no legal papers and no business on an individual's property, yet they set up their house on his territory.

And if allowed to squat for too long, they bring a possessing force within him. People actually "possess" the spirit of oppression, which suffocates and causes them to worry about everything—and all because they granted them access to their land.

When people "possess" the spirit of depression, it can cause them to cry all the time. Depression produces mood swings that cause them to feel as if no one loves or cares for them. Ultimately, they begin to show physical signs of oppression through sickness, and in some cases they become hypochondriacs. All of these bad seeds begin to blossom and take form because of a demonic oppressive spirit operating in their lives.

Satan strategizes all of it very carefully—so at a time when people should be possessing the land and walking in the blessings of God, they end up overwhelmed and possessed by the circumstances of life. Suddenly, they are idle—and you know the old saying: "An idle mind is the devil's workshop." So Satan continues to diligently work away. Once oppression and depression make a place for possession, this stronghold causes its victims to lose all self-control and become slaves to the oppressing force that holds them captive. Following is the story of one such possessed man.

Though the Scriptures give many stories of demon possession, one story that stands out in particular is found in Mark 5:1-11. In this story, there was a man possessed by a legion of unclean spirits that gave him such physical strength no one could restrain him.

> *And always, night and day, he was in the mountains and in the tombs, crying out and cutting himself with stones. But when he saw Jesus from afar, he ran and worshiped Him.*

> *And he cried out with a loud voice and said, "What have I to do with You, Jesus, Son of the Most High God? I implore You by God that You do not torment me"* (Mark 5:5-7).

Upon recognizing Jesus, these oppressive spirits immediately understood that they could no longer reign in this man's life as they had for so long. So they made an earnest appeal to Jesus to not send them out of the country.

In verse 9, Jesus asked the unclean spirit:

> *"What is your name?" And he answered, saying, "My name is Legion; for we are many." And he begged him earnestly that He would not send them out of the country. Now a large herd of swine was there feeding near the mountains. And all the demons begged him, saying, "Send us to the swine, that we may enter them." And at once Jesus gave them permission. Then the unclean spirits went out and entered the swine (there were about two thousand); and the herd ran violently down the steep place into the sea, and drowned in the sea* (verses 10-13).

This story, which ends in victory, provides incredible revelation concerning the fierceness of a possessing demonic spirit. This passage of Scripture confirms that possession can indeed drive a human being to dwell in caves like a madman.

The Many Names of Oppression

Oppression, however, has many names: boredom, loneliness, alienation, criticism, racism, arrogance ...these are only some of oppression's aliases. Even though under normal circumstances these circumstances can be relieved, or even cured, when the spirit of oppression is in operation, no natural means can permanently lift its weight.

Boredom and loneliness, for instance, can *normally* be satisfied by the company of others. But when one is oppressed by these demonic forces, relationship with others is stifled. An oppressed person can be in a crowded room filled with jubilant people, yet still feel the heaviness of boredom and loneliness upon their shoulders.

Some oppressive spirits tend to surface in a person because he was the recipient of the bad seeds of an oppressor—such as I was through Ms. Thomas's cutting words. Past traumas and criticisms passed along through bad teaching and oppressive people have produced racism and other social stumbling blocks that have millions bound.

The next time you feel bored and you realize that this boredom can't be satisfied by watching a movie, or by conversation or companionship, be advised that this is an oppressive spirit.

If you're being criticized and this causes you to be ultra-critical of yourself—thinking that nothing you do is right, and causing you to feel like a failure—take notice immediately that this is a spirit and that it can be very destructive. Know that supernatural forces are in operation and that there is nothing natural about these situations. Know also that these spirits will destroy you if the necessary steps aren't taken to bind them and keep them from operating in your life.

Boredom, criticism, racism, inferiority—note these common names. They could be symptoms of an oppressive spirit. And if they come to plunder you, hit the floor in prayer. Pray this prayer now, if you need to be loosed from oppression's grip:

Father, in the name of Jesus, I take authority over every oppressive spirit that is trying to operate in my life. I denounce the spirits of boredom, criticism, racism, and all other inferiority complexes that come to hinder my growth in Christ. No longer will I allow myself to be bound, but I will exercise the authority that You have given me to bind the hand of the enemy.

According to 1 John 4:3, I know that greater is He who is in me, than he who is in the world. So I submit myself to You and Your power, and I will no longer allow the enemy to have free reign and rule over my life.

I thank You now, Father, that even as I pray in faith, I am being loosed from the bonds of oppression. I am free from darkness, and I am now liberated into Your marvelous light. I give You the glory for the miracle You have just performed within my life! Amen.

4

ADDICTION

Oppression's Deceptive Road To Escape

Addiction is the spirit of oppression's most deceptive road to escape. Addiction carries with it a very blatant and overwhelmingly destructive power. But it can manifest with such subtleness that one hardly knows he's locked into it—until it's too late.

To gain an understanding of what addiction really is, let's first define it. *Addiction* means "habitually engaging in an act with no self-control." No matter how hard an addicted individual tries, he can't seem to break the chains that hold him captive. Though some addicted people try to get free on occasion, they find that they don't have the strength or will to "kick the habit." They discover that they are trapped—forced to continually engage in the addictive act.

Temptation: Addiction's Root

The root of all addiction is first temptation, which comes from Satan, who preys on the weaknesses of an individual by setting the bait. The enemy very readily knows what to send at what particular time because we often exhibit our strengths and weaknesses in the way we govern our lives. This gives him place to continually tempt us, and if possible, addict us.

Temptation will come, but God will always provide a way of escape.

> *No temptation has overtaken you except such as is common to man; but God is faithful, who will not allow you to be tempted beyond what you are able, but with the temptation will also make the way of escape, that you may be able to bear it* (1 Corinthians 10:13).

And when His way of escape is presented, the decision to either run for the exit or continue to satisfy the flesh can often mean the difference between life or death.

God won't make the decision for us. He gives us clarity of mind through scriptural truth and counsels us on the biblical decision. But He leaves the decision in the hands of the one who is wrestling with the addiction.

> *"I call heaven and earth as witnesses today against you, that I have set before you life and death, blessing and cursing; therefore choose life, that both you and your descendants may live"* (Deuteronomy 30:19).

The Lord himself was tempted, but He resisted—providing us with an example of overcoming faith. Jesus met every one of Satan's temptations with the quoted Word of God.

> *Then Jesus, being filled with of the Holy Spirit, returned from the Jordan and was led by the Spirit into the wilderness, being tempted forty days by the devil. And in those days He ate nothing, and afterward when they had ended, He was hungry. And the devil said to Him, "If*

> *You are the Son of God, command this stone to become bread." But Jesus answered him, saying, "***It is written***, 'Man shall not live by bread alone, but by every word of God'"* (Luke 4:1-4).

Jesus could have done anything within His power to ward off Satan's temptations at this point of His life. Later, in the Garden of Gethsemane, he told Peter that he could call for twelve legions of angels to deal with the Roman soldiers, but it wasn't God's will. God's will in Jesus' wilderness temptation was to show the power of His Word over the tempter. And when Jesus persisted, the devil *...departed from Him until an opportune time* (Luke 4:13).

Faith in God's Word and an individual's desire for deliverance is God's way of temptation's escape. Those who allow Satan's snares to eventually addict them need to seek God and grow in faith.

Addiction not only affects the one who is a slave to it but also affects those whom the individual is closest to in relationship. When a person gives in to the tactics and temptations of Satan, he becomes a slave to the "thing" that was used as bait to tempt him.

The Many Names of Addiction

Addiction comes in many forms and is disguised by many different names: drug addiction, chemical abuse, and sexual addiction—which in itself has many titles...nymphomania, homosexuality, and sodomy, to name a few. Then there are lying and stealing addictions, which we often refer to as compulsive behavioral disorders, and so on.

Whatever the name, it can all be summed up in one word—**addiction**. So powerful are some addictions that the majority of a person's life can be spent trying to break free while continually falling deeper into the same snare.

As a young boy growing up on the hard streets of New York City, I found out first hand the painful struggles of trying to loose oneself from the bonds of addiction. My desire to escape the abject poverty and dangers of my tough neighborhood overrode my desire to resist when offered the temporal escape of drugs. As a result, what began as a "one-time" experience to escape the oppressive thoughts of my mind and the traumas that I endured daily, soon evolved into a $270-per-day cocaine habit. So strong was the addiction that I, the one who was oppressed, soon began to oppress others to satisfy my need. I robbed and stole whatever it took to get the drugs I needed to relieve the pain of my addiction.

But as I look back today, I can see that God, in the midst of my addiction and oppressive behavior, gave His angels charge over me (see Psalm 91:11) so He might receive glory out of my life.

The road to God's glory led me first to Rikers Island Prison in New York City. While there, I was forced to abide within a new and overpowering oppressive environment. Suddenly, all the courage I'd used to torment and take from others disappeared, and I felt hollow, alone—oppressed.

It was while I was in this state of nothingness that God showed up and not only ministered to me but set me free in my mind...and also from prison.

Today I stand as a living testimony of John 8:36, *"Therefore if the Son makes you free, you shall be free indeed."* I gladly return unto God a debt that can never be fully paid, by preaching His Word all over the world and testifying of His liberating power and authority over every oppressive spirit, including addiction.

Oppression is *a spirit* that produces addiction's deadly force. This is why the world has so often failed in its attempts to free addicts through its techniques of rehabilitation. Because the world can't approach deliverance through the agency of God's power, those who do eventually break free of a habit through secular therapies find themselves continually harassed by the spirit of addiction that constantly knocks at their door. These strongholds are demonic outposts that can only be removed by weapons of spiritual force as mentioned in 2 Corinthians 10:4.

Oppression is persistent. So it continually knocks until the one who has "kicked their habit" becomes too weak to bear the temptation and falls prey again to the lies of the devil. The spirit of addiction lies to its victim, saying, "One more time won't hurt," when in fact "one more time" can actually kill him.

Every twelve-step program for addiction is set up with natural checks and balances to help the addicted person avoid impending falls. When tempted, they are instructed to call their program sponsor. But if he or she isn't home, or if the addict chooses not to call, the spirit of addiction moves in again to undo any progress that may have been achieved.

Sobriety, or abstinence, is the aim of these admirable programs, but to be sober is to struggle continually to stay addiction free. Many have survived through these techniques, and are to be commended. But one day of spiritual deliverance is worth more than a lifetime of difficult sobriety.

The world teaches, "once an addict, always an addict."

The Bible teaches, *"...if the Son makes you free, you shall be free indeed."*

Society teaches the techniques of "mind over matter" and "will power" to conquer addictions.

The Word of God teaches, *"My strength is made perfect in* [your] *weakness"* (2 Corinthians 12:9).

Much of a person's life can be wasted and ruined by idly playing around in the enemy's territory, never gaining total deliverance from a habit that carries a price that none can afford to pay. Addictive habits kill multiplied thousands every year and disable thousands of others. Those who have achieved twelve-step lifestyles of sobriety are to be commended. But when you talk to many of them, you realize that they really aren't free. Members in Alcoholics Anonymous meetings traditionally address the group by affirming their alcoholism. "Hi, my name is John, and I'm an alcoholic." So they are sober, but they are still living "one drink"—or "one fix"—away from their achieved sobriety.

God knows that once the enemy entangles an individual within the webs of addiction, it takes His strength to gain full deliverance. He knows that the human will is weak and that without His power operating in a person's life, he is no match for the oppressive spirit that seeks to destroy him. But God's Word and Spirit conquered death and the grave. And if His power accomplished that, you can be sure that it is His desire to conquer sniveling little devils who are under militaristic assignment to snare whomever they can with this or that addiction!

Because addiction is oppression's most deceptive road to escape, freedom gained spiritually will be challenged. And those who aren't aware of Satan's tactics could easily lose everything.

Amy's Story

As a teenager, Amy's home life was very different from that of her friends at school. Many of them placed her on a pedestal, but they had no idea of the turmoil and struggle she faced day after day when she went home.

Because of her parent's financial pressures, Amy returned home from school daily to a very oppressive home—never knowing what kind of mood her parents might be in when she arrived. So she began skipping school, dating guys much older than herself, staying out late, and ultimately began experimenting with drugs and alcohol.

Amy could see this road to destruction, and for a time she was able to break free. She lived through a period in her life when everything seemed to be going well. She appeared to be living a very prosperous and satisfying life. But after a time, she was visited again—as Satan invariably does—by these same temptations. But this time he was playing for keeps!

The devil knew that although Amy had been dealt a bad hand in life, still she knew the Word and how to apply the power of prayer. So Amy was a definite threat to him, and he intended to wipe her out...just as the devil departed from Jesus "until a more opportune time" (see Luke 4:13). So he returned to Amy.

But Amy wasn't as victorious as Jesus in conquering her temptations this time. They soon enslaved and overpowered her in the form of addictions.

First of all, because of her past experiences with older and more experienced men, Amy's tendency to feel incomplete without this kind of men in her life made her a slave to sexual perversion. She became a slave not only to sex but to the men as well—and through them, she became enslaved to alcohol and drugs.

Eventually Amy's addictions forced her to give up all that she had, including her own children. She couldn't break free in her own strength, and she did unmentionable things to get her next fix.

Amy's friends became her enemies, and her loved ones became her competitors. And in her enslaved mind, she was convinced that everyone was falsely accusing her—that they were out to get her. She felt that everyone was wrong except Amy.

Unfortunately, Amy's quest to find victory continued to lead to nothing but defeat. Her own will was too weak to war against the attacks Satan consistently used to overwhelm her. And because she was deceived into thinking God no longer listened to her prayers, she refused to invoke the power of God in her life in order to be set free. Today, Amy's loved ones continue to pray to God on her behalf that total deliverance shall be her portion. However, the ultimate decision depends totally on Amy's desire to be set free—not only from drug addiction but from the oppressive spirit that Satan has launched against her life.

This is a good example of how addiction not only destroys the body but also clouds and corrupts the mind. But those who keep their minds on God's Word receive His peace and stay free from Satan's lies:

> *You will keep him in perfect peace, whose mind is stayed on You, because he trusts in You* (Isaiah 26:3).

Getting your mind off the things of God and onto the lusts of the flesh is an open door for Satan to slither through. If given enough access, He will barge in and steal the promises that God has ordained for your life. Only God can keep your mind in perfect peace, but He can only do it when your mind is stayed on Him. He places before you life and death—but the choice is yours!

Because sexual sin is the only potential downfall of a Christian that Paul instructs the New Testament church to "flee from" (see 1 Corinthians 6:18), I have devoted the entire next chapter to the subject. But whatever the addiction may be, we can't find victory in our own strength. As Paul describes in Romans 7:15-20, our flesh becomes a trap, and we find ourselves desiring to do good, but the sin within us habitually draws us into doing the things we hate.

> *For what I am doing, I do not understand. For what I will to do, that I do not practice; but what I hate, that I do. If, then, I do what I will not to do, I agree with the law that it is good. But now, it is no longer I who do it, but sin that dwells in me. For I know that in me (that is, in my flesh) nothing good dwells; for to will is present with me, but how to perform what is good I do not find. For the good that I will to do, I do not do; but the evil I will not to do, that I practice. Now if I do what I will not to do, it is no longer I who do it, but sin that dwells in me.*

As this passage in Romans indicates, because only the spirit of man is saved when the blood of Jesus sets him free, the body continues to war against God's will. The body is still flesh and will remain so until the judgment day. So what we often want to do according to the conviction of the Holy Spirit and the commandments of God's Word, we fail to do. Instead, we find ourselves doing the very thing that we said we'd never do.

As Paul states, it is no longer we who do it but sin that abides within us. So we must approach the spirit and the fear that accompanies it with boldness and faith. God's Word will devour our enemy but we must believe this.

This is why the spirit of addiction must be approached as just that—a spirit. In order to fight off the addiction and find peace and victory, we must approach the battle spiritually and we must be well equipped with God's Word.

Addicted Saints

Although we tend to think of addictions as being prevalent mainly in the outside world, many saints fail to address or even acknowledge the addictions that take place within the church.

Addictions such as eating disorders and overeating that lead to obesity and other health problems exist within the church. When the trials and tests of life come, many turn to their food addiction, instead of to Christ, as a way of escape. At a time when some should be turning away from the plate to fast and seek God, they feed the flesh to satisfy a void that can only be quenched by God.

Satan often uses food as a distraction when God is trying to get our attention. The devil knows when our will is weak in this area. So when we find ourselves restless, with God trying to provoke us into His Word and fellowship, the first thing we run to is the refrigerator.

There we find that even after we've eaten, the restlessness remains, so we eat again and again until we're finally too full to even think of picking up God's Word or having a time of fellowship with Him. So the temptation, the bait, the addiction, all work together for one common goal—destruction.

Gluttony

Gluttony is a spirit of want—not need. It is a demon that operates through depression and oppression. My mention of this addiction, however, isn't intended to force anyone into some kind of unplanned diet.

Many churches have advocated what I believe is a demonic "doctrine of health" that stresses how much weight a person should put on or take off. Many saints are now hooked on diet pills, which is another form of substance abuse, because of this kind of teaching. Others go on food binges to put on weight. Here is Ms. Smith's story.

I knew a lady some time ago who routinely spent her day sitting on her porch watching soap operas while she shaved carrots, snapped beans, and seasoned meats for her family's dinner. She was very friendly and waved at everyone who passed her way.

Everyone who knew this lady loved and respected her as a spiritual woman. She never used profanity, never smoked cigarettes, and never participated in any of the local parties. But two things stood out about her: she was considerably overweight, and she never went to church.

Even on special occasions such as Christmas, Easter, Mother's Day, and so on, when non-Christians went to church, Ms. Smith would stay home, comfortably going about her daily routine. She even had many god-children, but she would never participate in any of their dedication services.

Why? Because Ms. Smith had been taught by her pastor that those who were overweight were lazy sluggards. She had been convinced that overweight Christians didn't have faith and that God couldn't love anyone who allowed themselves to look this way.

So Ms. Smith sought to correct her woeful situation. But as a result of trying a variety of weight-loss techniques, she experienced numerous medical problems. She even subjected herself to such techniques as stomach stapling and having her mouth wired partially shut. This ultimately caused her to go into cardiac arrest. God mercifully spared her life, but the pain she endured emotionally damaged her permanently.

No one in her congregation, including the pastor, paid Ms. Smith a visit while she was in the hospital. To them, her condition was not a real medical problem. They just assumed she was weak and lacked proper faith. But little did they know that they themselves had departed from the faith, and that the seducing, oppressing spirits that were ruling their church put them in the condition spoken of in 1 Timothy 4:1,2:

> *Now the Spirit expressly says that in latter times some will depart from the faith, giving heed to seducing spirits and doctrines of demons, speaking lies in hypocrisy, having their own conscience seared with a hot iron.*

In America we're always eating. At every "special occasion" there is a mountain of food to celebrate the joyous occasion. At most wedding receptions there is an abundance of food. Even when someone dies—the first thing the grieving family receives from friends and loved ones is food. So food is always with us, and oppression will tempt those who will take it to extremes.

We need to be reminded that Jesus knows we're all different and that we each have our own levels of contentment and dissatisfaction. There is a tremendous amount of cultural expectations placed on slimness today, so we must be careful about making people conform to this image that is satisfactory to society. Some people feel good about their weight and have good self-esteem. So they should in no way be forced to lose weight based upon what is most appealing to the eyes of society. Then there are those who, because of coming out of other addictions such as drugs, sexual perversion, and so on, tend to cling to food as a source of comfort. These should be helped to recognize oppression's replacement in the area of gluttony. Everyone would do well to remember Matthew 7:1, which says, *"Judge not, that you be not judged"* (Matthew 7:1).

We all know that it's good to use wisdom in what we eat, but one should never fall under the oppressive spirit of a pastor or any other person in an effort to measure up to what the world statistically views as the norm of ideal weight. Unfortunately, Ms. Smith never returned to church, and she died in her home while her children were away. They found her three days after she had died of a heart attack. I personally believe it was an "attack" on her heart due to the oppression of emotional damage that had been suppressed for so long.

Today, hundreds of thousands of other women are sitting in dark rooms somewhere finding comfort in food because of miscarriages, broken relationships, past traumas or whatever the case may be. You will find thousands of men eating their way to "fulfillment" as well.

From what I've learned, to the food addict, food is a friend. It has a wonderful aroma, it doesn't judge, it comes to dinner, it goes to the theater, and it subliminally soothes the mind during difficult times. This is why we must understand that addiction, no matter what form it comes in, is destructive. No good thing can ever come out of it. Addiction comes to rob our health and sanity and to oppress those who love us.

Finally, no matter how strong a force any addiction may seem, freedom from addiction simply lies within the power of prayer. If you happen to be one who is held captive by oppressive destructive behavior that is beyond your control, your only means of escape is to invoke the power of God in your life through sincere prayer and continual fellowship with Him. So I offer the following prayer as a starting point. If you pray it sincerely, you can believe that God's Holy Spirit will begin imparting His strength to set you free:

Heavenly Father, in the name of Jesus, I submit all of my soul, my body, my desires, and my emotions to You and to Your Spirit. I denounce any conscious or subconscious addictive tendencies formed in my past. I denounce the emotional, physical, and spiritual ties formed by my involvement in any unhealthy habits. I thank You for forgiving and cleansing me of all unrighteousness, right now! I loose myself from all ties to past relationships that were formed to keep me tied to my addictions.

Please uproot all connections through dependencies, perversions, and enslaving thoughts that hold me captive and oppressed. I bind every evil spirit that reinforced addiction in my life through ungodly associations and temptations.

Lord, I ask You to cleanse my mind and to erase totally from my soulish desires all illicit habitual acts. Set me free so that I may serve only the purposes of God and walk into the divine destiny that You have preordained for my life.

Father, now that I have asked You this, knowing that it is in accordance with Your will for my life, I believe I am totally forgiven and set free. I commit myself to You—mind, soul, and body—in Jesus' name. Amen

In praying this prayer with a genuine heart and sincerity, "old things are passed away," and you may now walk in your new life. Old friends and acquaintances may still remember and remind you of old habits in passing, but God is not a man. Your slate is now clean. So continue to pray daily and fellowship with the Lord to stay free from temptation. Walk in liberty and be free from the oppressive yoke of addiction!

5

SEXUALLY TRANSMITTED DECEPTIONS AND SPIRITS

(STDs)

As I pointed out in the previous chapter, the sin of sexual immorality is the only potential downfall that Paul commanded the church to flee from in 1 Corinthians 6:18. So, in a book such as this, I think I would be negligent at best to avoid some detail on the subject of sex.

If you don't think sexual temptation has been used by Satan to destroy the work of God over the last two decades, you haven't read many newspapers or watched TV.

Sexuality, which was given by God for the sole purpose of pleasure within the covenant bonds of marriage and for the reproduction of life, can also carry with it a very strong oppressive and destructive spirit. We all possess the emotions of sexuality within, which is why certain guidelines of discipline must be maintained in order to refrain from falling prey to our weaknesses in this area. Perhaps even more dangerous than the actual weakness is denying that these emotions actually exist.

> *Flee sexual immorality. Every sin that a man does is outside the body, but he who commits sexual immorality sins against his own body* (1 Corinthians 6:18).

The after-effects of many acts of sexual behavior can become the means of enslaving an individual to addictive habits. Those who engage in unbridled sexual appetites can become heir to various transmitted spirits and strongholds in life. Once this form of oppression takes root, healing must take place. Any sexual addiction healing process should consist not only of a daily medicinal intake of the Word of God, but abstinence from the addictive sin in order to insure the strength of the spiritual immune system.

To better understand the impact of sexual sins in comparison to spiritually transmitted illnesses that invade people to deceive them, let's first examine the consequences of sexual sins of the natural.

STDs
Sexually Transmitted Diseases

In today's promiscuous society, when two individuals come together in physical sexual intimacy, they risk illness from the transference of bodily fluids. Sexually transmitted diseases (STDs) are, alarmingly, quite common. Medical tracking and statistics report some thirteen million cases of these sorts of infections annually.

STDs
Spiritually Transferred Demons

But untracked, and unknown to most, are the spiritually transmitted diseases, deceptions, and spirits connected with sex. As it is in the natural, so it is in the spiritual. When a forbidden relationship and sexual connection is made, a price must always be paid.

Many times in forbidden relationships, a person may find himself struggling to let go of the constant urge to continue in sin with someone he has been intimately involved with. This is not uncommon, because when a man and woman become one and join their flesh, they not only experience moments of physical pleasure, but they also inherit a part of the other individual's spirit.

Oppression's tempting lie of "one time won't hurt" can be heard echoing throughout Satan's many forms of addictive temptations—but whatever the addiction, "one time" can ultimately kill.

A number of ungodly spirits can be transferred through the bond of sexual intimacy, such as greed, lust for power and wealth, and unfaithfulness, to name a few. The spirit of sexual oppression will attempt to deceive the one it tempts into thinking that he or she will walk away the same person they were before the act was committed. But this simply isn't the case.

> *Can a man take fire to his bosom, and his clothes not be burned? Can one walk on hot coals, and his feet not be seared? So he who goes in to his neighbor's wife; whoever touches her shall not be innocent* (Proverbs 6:27-29).

Both parties involved in an illicit sexual encounter will always walk away having acquired spirits that were once nonexistent, whether good or bad.

Lori's Story

Lori, who was in her early thirties, finally met "the man of her dreams." Both she and Jonathan were single, but this man was involved with another woman whom he planned to marry. Knowing the consequences of pursuing such a relationship, Lori fought hard to flee this man's grasp. But before long she succumbed to the delicate attentiveness that Jonathan showed toward her. Soon they became consumed with each other, and Lori weakened in her fight of resistance against his sexual attempts.

After becoming sexually involved with Jonathan, immediately a number of changes began to take place in Lori's life. Before having sex with him, Lori had been very meek and quiet. Jonathan was powerful, successful, and at times a bit overbearing. All of these traits were a part of Lori's attraction for him, even though they were totally nonexistent in her own life. But as these two became intimately "one," Lori's drive for success and power became increasingly stronger. Where she once had been very meek, and to some degree introverted, she suddenly found herself enjoying the company and conversation of others. Through the bond of sexual intimacy, Jonathan's spirit had been transferred to her. And eventually his spirit overwhelmed and governed her entire life.

Lori and Jonathan had both been deluded by oppression's illusion into thinking their sexual encounters were somehow justified. Then when the reality of their plight finally became a reality to Lori, they both began to pray—but to no avail. The more they tried to part, the more their desire to be in each other's presence drove them together. Everything about Jonathan—his hunger for success, his drive for perfection, and even a bit of his overbearing behavior—had infected Lori. Needless to say, they both had become the "thorn" in the other's flesh—wanting to walk in liberty, yet lacking the will and the "know how" to do so.

In time, however, victory eventually prevailed—but only through much discipline, prayer, and divine intervention from God. Although Jonathan and Lori both confess that temptation occasionally knocks at the door, they continue to apply the Word of God to their lives, which says, *Resist the devil and he will flee from you* (James 4:7). By denying their flesh in obedience to God, a vow was formed, symbolizing their commitment to Christ as being first and foremost in their lives. As a result, they've both been elevated spiritually and are currently pursuing very prosperous careers—walking in liberty, free from the bondage and guilt of willful sin.

Incubated Danger

Medically speaking, the time between infection and the actual physical appearance of infection is called the incubation period. The incubation period for the sexually transmitted disease called syphilis is normally about twenty-one days. This means that within its twenty-one day time frame, no precautions are being taken to insure the safety of the other individual. Neither is the infected person receiving proper medical care. Syphilis is silently growing and coming to fruition.

Even after the physical manifestation of syphilis surfaces, which appears as a painless sore, this physical evidence heals itself in one to five weeks. But that doesn't mean the disease has gone into remission. In fact, once the actual sore disappears, it gives a false hope of healing because the syphilis infection is still very much a reality.

Spiritually speaking, the same deceptive external realities are true within the infected transference of sexual spirits. Satan's greatest weapon is to plant the seed of sin in our hearts. Then he waits patiently for the incubation period to take place. He deceives his victims by producing the illusion of perfect health—when in fact, within their bodies, Satan's specialized spirits are just waiting for the right time to surface.

Physical evidence of illness will follow an encounter, but within a few weeks, it may appear to be nonexistent. Spiritually, this is Satan's way of deceiving an individual into thinking he is fine. At first, sexual partners may feel some strain and guilt—the result of the voice of their conscience. Then as time passes, they may feel relieved. What they don't understand is that the spiritual and physical immune systems of those who fall into sexual sin will be challenged or even destroyed. The hot coals spoken of in Proverbs 6:26,27 may grow dim for a while, but they don't burn out.

Sexual Strongholds

Once a sexual stronghold has been created, it takes more than prayer to bring forth deliverance. The habits in one's lifestyle must be changed, and the need to abstain from fleshly desires is an absolute must. Whatever the source of the stronghold, it must become the target of attack if the stronghold is to be broken. Ignorance in this area only further handicaps and enslaves anyone who honestly desires to be set free.

In cases such as Lori and Jonathan's, where sexual intimacy creates a soul tie, the only means of breaking this addictive spirit is by prayer and fasting and by abstaining from further sexual encounters. But before any of this can become reality, one must have the desire to be set free. Honesty with oneself and God is a definite must because only then can true repentance spring forth. But an individual should never repent for something he is not yet willing to release. "Unrepentant repentance" will eventually produce a reprobate mind, endangering the one so deluded with a continual life of sin.

Perversion and Promiscuity

Two of the most common problems that can develop out of sexually transmitted spirits are perversion and promiscuity. The formation of a soul tie through the bondage of promiscuity is, in most cases, extraordinarily hard to break. This is because the soul of the promiscuous individual is scattered among a host of mates, all of whom have contributed their own individual oppressive spirits into this one person. Women, especially, because of their sensitive emotional makeup, find that soul ties birthed out of promiscuity are extremely binding. As a result, they, more than men, find themselves habitually falling into the clutches of previous mates and sex partners whom they declared they would never see again. Again, all of this can result from soul ties that were specifically formed out of lust. They work to keep the one in bondage enslaved to a life of constant instability.

> *...do you not know that he who is joined to a harlot is one body with her? For "The two," He*

says, "shall become one flesh" (1 Corinthians 6:16).

Neither are men exempt from this kind of bondage to promiscuity. So strong is the soul tie of some men to previous partners that they mentally engage in acts of reconsummating sex acts they had with former mates. So, the destructive results of promiscuity in both women and men can continually risk their well-being, causing them to be drawn to previous partners—long after the relationships have been severed.

The Sexually Transferred Demon of Homosexuality

Another destructive soul tie that can be sexually transmitted is homosexuality. Many cases of homosexuality are transmitted through past sexual molestation that occurred in childhood. When this sort of perverted violation occurs, not only is a child's innocence ripped away, but unbeknownst to the child, the will to be set free is also taken.

So strong are the oppressive ties of homosexuality, that few are able to find deliverance and freedom from a slave-driven, ongoing struggle. In addition to prayer, the person deceived and oppressed by this sexually perverted spirit, must engage in ongoing godly counsel. There is a particularly strong need to reinforce the rejection of former sexual habits while establishing new behaviors when ministering to former homosexuals. Exodus International, a tremendous Christian organization made up of former homosexuals, promotes these kind of small group meetings that are necessary to adequately deal with the homosexual spirit.

The greatest deceiving factor in coming to delivering terms with homosexuality is denial. In order to be set free, one must first identify and acknowledge that the problem exists. The greatest weapon against Satan's arsenal of deception is information and confrontation. But many times, even as parents, we tend to cover up the real issues. We sometimes tend to deceive ourselves into thinking our child will "grow out of it," and by so doing, we give free reign to the enemy.

Any time there are past occurrences of sexual perversion or promiscuity within a family, the maturing of these traits can manifest in generations to come. Children will sometimes unknowingly act out the lifestyles of their family as the latest transmitters of their family's generational curses. If you ever happen to be put in a position to minister to such a child, the spirit that is in operation must be denounced through the blood of Jesus if deliverance is to take place. Of course, always remember to use wisdom so as not to frighten the child, who in most cases is totally oblivious to what is taking place.

There must always be a balance as well as consistency in dealing with this kind of abuse.

Alex's Story

Because of the shame Alex endured through molestation, he never confronted the new feelings he started to experience in being attracted to men. Although his mother saw the development of these traits, she felt that her son was just "going through a phase" and would eventually grow out of it. However, by the time Alex reached adulthood, his mother was finally praying for freedom from his condition because he had totally "come out of the closet."

Alex the adult saw no need to seek the freedom his mother now desired for him, so he continued freely in his homosexual acts. Alex was set free by the power of God for a brief period, but because he didn't exercise discipline and seek continued godly counsel, he soon fell prey to his old lifestyle. This time, however, Alex was visited by seven worse demons, and he became even more lawless in his perversion. This soul tie had become a yoke around his neck that was much too heavy for him to manage.

After years of wandering, Alex finally returned to the fellowship of the church. Nonetheless, he continues to struggle with the curse of this aggressive spirit of homosexuality. His family, however, understands the power of prayer and continues to pray that the Lord will deliver Alex so he may enjoy the liberty of a true relationship with Christ. Alex's story serves as a sobering reminder of the importance of staying free once one has been set free by the power of God. Studying the Bible, spending time in prayer, and attending a church that provides good spiritual food are *musts* if one is to maintain victory and avoid the struggles Alex encountered.

Untying the Knots That Bind

In order to undo the damage of a soul tie, a spiritual untying must take place. The power of loosing and binding must be exercised.

> *"And I will give you the keys of the kingdom of heaven, and whatever you bind on earth will be bound in heaven, and whatever you loose on earth will be loosed in heaven"* (Matthew 16:19).

Knots that have been illegally formed in our lives don't have the authority to reign in our lives. Bondage to soul ties should never be taken lightly or ignored, but should be considered as life or death situations and be viewed with the severity described by Paul in 1 Corinthians 6:9,10:

> *Do you not know that the unrighteous will not inherit the kingdom of God? Do not be deceived. Neither fornicators, nor idolaters, nor adulterers, nor homosexuals, nor sodomites, nor thieves, nor covetous, nor drunkards, nor revilers, nor extortioners will inherit the kingdom of God.*

None of us can afford to be sexually deceived. Satan's oppressive spirit of sexual destruction is at work in the church today. Can you think of a minister—famous or local—who shipwrecked his ministry because of giving in to the lust of the flesh? Have you heard of any Christian divorce cases that came about through infidelity? You probably have.

The enemy uses his sexually transmitted spirits and deceptions to destroy the ministry God has predestined for each individual. Satan knows that the seed God has planted within His people will grow into maturity to touch the lives of many others, so he subtly uses sexual temptations as a means of distraction to try to get God's people off track and keep them away from the things of God. Those he can lure, he does—to the point of death if they allow it. But praise be to God for those who have their mind and vision firmly planted in God's Word. Satan can't deceive these folks, so he will have to look elsewhere to create his next sexual deviant!

If you have been snared through the power of illicit sex or are being tempted now to become involved in it, I tell you the same thing Paul said in 1 Corinthians 6:18—Run! Run to God for clarity of mind and the reality of what the deceptive encounter will eventually produce—hot coals, misery, and possibly death.

God never repents for the gift he places within us, but He allows His mercy to rest upon us. No cry is too meaningless for Him to soothe and no sin is too great for Him to forgive. You can be set free from sexual sins by His power and anointing. So if you have been dealing with this type of oppressive sexual attack, I invite you to pray the following prayer of deliverance.

Father God, in the name of Jesus Christ, I ask You to forgive me for sexual sins. I ask for courage to admit my faults to all concerned. I am Yours, a holy person. So Holy Father, please give me a new revelation of my holy purity, and set me free. I confess and believe John 8:36 now, which says, ***If the Son makes you free, you shall be free indeed****. I am holy and I am pure! Because You are living in me, I am free! And I give You all the praise and glory. Amen*

Now, to ensure your change of lifestyle and to maintain your newfound freedom and walk in victory, study 1 Corinthians 6 very closely—then be sensitive to God's Spirit concerning what to do next.

6

SATAN'S NEW OPPRESSION

"Hotlines" to Deadly Deception

Blessed is the man Who walks not in the counsel of the ungodly... (Psalm 1:1).

Before concluding this book on oppression, I need to point out the alarming explosion of witchcraft that is occurring today through America's new psychic TV hotlines. For those who succumb to what many would humorously blow off as a rip-off fortune telling, an addiction for intimate, hidden knowledge can set in.

First of all, the Word of God is very clear in stating where to get counsel and what kind of company to keep if we are to keep our spirits pure. But the following testimony reveals the reality and dangers behind the media personalities who televise and publicize their numbers by the thousands across the U.S.

Psychic hotline programs and magazine numbers have been connecting the curious and oppressed (both in and out of the church) with the oppressor himself in startling, growing numbers. Here is one woman's testimony.

Hooked by the Hotline

"One night while up 'channel surfing' on the television, I stumbled upon one of the psychic network shows. I quickly turned away from it, but I turned right back to it because the psychic on the screen had tapped into things that intrigued me. This began a weekly habit of calls, with bills of $10 to $20 per week, which would eventually increase as my desire for more information increased. As time went on, I dialed more and more numbers and paid more and more money, because for me, this meant more in-depth information.

"Finally, at about the third level of my seeking, I heard a very pleasant voice on the other end of the phone that I immediately felt a closeness to. She gave me a strange kind of "knowing" within, and I felt I could trust her with the deepest depths of my innermost secrets and soulish desires. The psychic's name was Crystal, and as I gave her my time, money, and ear, she told me all there was to know about myself.

"Upon answering my call and introducing herself, Crystal first asked me my date of birth. Then she asked me to repeat my name three times. Ten minutes into the conversation I was hooked. I was totally in awe of the things being revealed to her concerning my life. And the accuracy of this woman who just a few minutes earlier was a total stranger astounded me.

"Crystal knew of the fourteen-year-old abused teenager I was when growing up—and of the thirty-three year old who had lost almost everything, including her mind. I had lost my family in a fire that was ruled as arson, and I wanted to know why and who would leave me without a family. I lost my mother, my brother, my husband, and my seven-month-old baby. Depression had set in on my life, and I was about to lose my mind.

"The nightmares were the worst. I dreamed of my husband in the fire, calling out my name, and as I reached for him, he disappeared in the smoke and flames. Watching mothers with their small children became torment for me because I longed to cuddle the baby I'd tragically lost. And although I wanted to mother again, I also longed to be mothered. I longed for someone to provide the same comfort I so missed from my mother.

"So in my desperation to find answers, I was willing to try just about anything that would give me liberty and bring back life as I had once known it.

"Crystal provided me with the answers I felt I needed to restore my life. And the more I spoke with her, the more I felt anxiety building up in me to continue speaking with her and gaining her insights. So fascinated and intrigued was I that my heart palpitations increased with excitement, my palms became sweaty as I spoke, and I found myself approaching every new call like an addict going after the next fix.

"Soon, my life revolved around the counsel and direction of Crystal's insight. And before long, I couldn't even consider making a decision without consulting her.

"Crystal eventually told me that by providing her with my phone number she could introduce me to a psychic counselor who could better help me with some of the unanswered questions that still plagued my mind."

Seven Years of Black Magic

"I gladly received Crystal's offer and agreed to make contact with this 'local' psychic counselor. In fact, I was excited, because by now I had become totally engrossed in the mysticism of the psychic realm. My visit would plunge me into seven years of black magic, necromancy, heavy satanic enchantments, praying to ancient spirits, and eventually joining a school for witches, from which I graduated with honors before joining a witch's coven.

"All of this began from a TV psychic hotline that seemed to be so innocent. My minor fascinations with horoscopes, palm readings, or anything mystical that would catch my attention had finally turned into this.

"Once a part of the coven, I learned of a power that I'd never known I had, and I was fascinated by it. I had the power to make people do things against their will, and I loved it! As I progressed, I learned to administer my power of control through spell castings, love potions, hate potions, and separation and accident potions. I could even look into the heart of an individual and tell what they were thinking, then use that information in controlling their lives."

Free at Last

"This practice of oppressive manipulation and witchcraft ruled and reigned in my life for seven years. Then one night, a girlfriend of mine who was one of those born-again, Pentecostal, tongue-talking believers invited me to a tent meeting to hear an evangelist. He was one of those who claimed to have the power of God to cast out demons. At first I declined her invitation. But everyone in town was talking about this man, so I eventually decided to go.

"When the evangelist called me out of the crowd at the meeting, the demon that had taken up residence in my body for seven long years didn't intend to give up easily. But it was no match against the authority and blood of Christ...and as the man of God prayed and commanded it to come out, I was set free."

The preceding testimony is not only one of deliverance and liberty, but is also a commentary on Satan's deception in one of his most popular, mass-media forms. This woman, whose oppressing circumstances drove her to depression, also drove her to connect with Satan through his deceptive offers of hope.

You may say, "I'd never call one of those numbers." And you probably wouldn't. But this woman did. And so have many others within the church. Because it's out there on the television set and in magazine ads in soaring numbers, I mention this simply to show oppression's new high-tech psychic outreach, and to warn you about what it can do to a life.

The evangelist who came to this woman's town was me. When I was led to call her forward the night of the meeting, I had no idea of the battle that was awaiting me. While speaking into her life as the power of God overwhelmed me, this woman's entire countenance and demeanor transformed before my eyes. Her head was bowed down. Then as she slowly lifted it, I could see Satan's hate within her eyes. The demon was letting me know that he had overtaken her and was not going to come out just because I said to do so. Her eyes peered at me with the most gruesome satanic force I had ever seen as the voice of her demon spoke to me:

"YOU come to do war with me, you drug addict?" the demon hissed.

The oppressor sought to oppress me through my failures of my past. And when he did, I must admit that fear gripped me. But God was in control, and He began to remind me in a powerful way that this fight had nothing to do with me.

So I stood in the authority God had given me, looked this demon right in the face, and proclaimed, "I was once a drug addict—but I am no more. I've been bought by the blood of the Lamb and, in the name of Jesus, I command you to COME OUT!"

Realizing that he was defeated, this demon screeched a horrifying scream and immediately came out of this woman. She is now ministering the Word of God and is being used to bring deliverance to hundreds of people who were bound as she once was. Oppression had bound her in a witches coven, and it all began through a seemingly frivolous TV psychic hotline.

Are you following me? The TV psychic she spoke to separated her from any potential counsel except that of a psychic counselor who eventually led her to personal contact with a satanic cult. And it all started with this woman's oppression.

> *For though we walk in the flesh, we do not war according to the flesh. For the weapons of our warfare are not carnal but mighty in God for pulling down strongholds, casting down arguments and every high thing that exalts itself against the knowledge of God, bringing every thought into captivity to the obedience of Christ* (2 Corinthians 10:3-5).

As extreme as this woman's case may seem, her situation really isn't that uncommon to the less outward work of satanic oppression already discussed in this book. Remember the sequence:

1. Oppressing outward circumstance.
2. Depression.
3. Separation, and if possible, destruction.

The oppressing circumstance of this woman's fire was tragic. She lost her family in a house fire. Then depression set in and she slumped into hopelessness. Then Crystal was there—and this woman graduated with honors from Demon U! And she finally became an active oppressing member of the oppressor's local cult, where she was used—like Crystal—to control other people's lives.

Oppression is Oppression

Now, I don't claim to chase demons or venture out on witch-hunts. But the ministry the Lord has given me does involve setting the captives free through the authority of God's written Word. This authority will free the oppressed one who is hiding out from life in low self-esteem. And it will bring liberty to the drug, alcohol, food, sex, and psychic/mystic addict who is trying to escape from life.

I can't express strongly enough the spiritual warfare and deceptions that Satan is working against the minds of God's people today. He comes subtly to kill, steal, and destroy through past abuse, hopelessness, addiction, and focused lies.

Psychic hotlines are just one of the avenues that can lead the oppressed to destruction. It's not just entertainment. Tell your friends!

There are also many other forms of deadly and demon-driven deceptions in the world of occultism and witchcraft. And even some of God's saints are drawn into this mysticism—some through ignorance and some through being overly objective and open. But once an individual begins surfing around the edge of the devil's territory, it's only a matter of time before he is snatched into satanic strongholds and demonic possession that seems almost too powerful to be broken.

But there is an answer—and His name is Jesus. He has all power in heaven and earth, and He can break the bonds of all evil deception. So whether you've been tempted by some seemingly innocent form of witchcraft...or whether you're in total bondage to it—Jesus can bring deliverance. Pray with me now.

Father God, in the name of Jesus, I come to You now, asking You to forgive me for my interest and/or involvement in the evil deception of witchcraft. I believe that You have the power to break the chains of this bondage, and I come to You now, asking You to bring total deliverance in my life. I also ask that You give me a new hunger for more of Your Word, and help me to spend more time in prayer and fellowship with You. Thank You for hearing and answering my prayer. Amen.

7

BREAKING THROUGH THE BARRIERS

Disobedience and Unbelief

As Christians, we often define *sin* as "behavior unbecoming of one who names the name of Christ and visibly defies the laws of church doctrine." Sins such as this include fornication, adultery, lying and so on. But these kinds of rebellious acts are really only the residue that sin leaves behind. Sin in its rawest form is any deviation from what you know to be the will of God. And oppression is a deviant spirit, so sin is its ultimate fruit.

Sin, or "knowing disobedience" to the will of God, begins as a thought in the mind. But as the flesh wars against the spirit, a sinful thought uncontrolled will ultimately manifest outwardly through rebellious actions in many different forms.

...to obey is better than sacrifice...For rebellion is as the sin of witchcraft... (1 Samuel 15:22,23).

In examining the sin of unbelief, we find a dangerous web of deception that draws one away from the covering of God. Even blasphemy, the most dreadful sin of all, is birthed out of unbelief. However, to commit this sin, one would have to experience unbelief in its rarest and most demonic form, because to have truly experienced the fullness of God and His power, would make it very difficult to turn from the truth. But the unbelief that comes through oppression certainly can cloud one's mind to the point that when God actually shows up, the individual won't even recognize Him.

For example, Jesus couldn't perform any miracles in Nazareth because of the people's unbelief. Israel was an oppressed people, and many had grown hardhearted with certain expectations. Jesus didn't fit their Messianic menu, so their unbelief produced condemnation, which will lead to spiritual death. With as much sickness and disease as there is in the world, there were probably many Jesus would have healed in Nazareth, which could have led to their spiritual life ...but instead, they proclaimed their own spiritual death.

If you're sick but don't believe God is still a healer, you will speak death to your healing. If you don't believe God provides prosperity to His people, you will speak death to your prosperity. Unbelief immediately causes you to forfeit what God said He can do in your life.

God is true to His Word. So if He said it, it shall be so. But if you want His will fulfilled in your life here on earth as it is already done in heaven, you must break down the barriers of unbelief. And one of these barrier's greatest contributors is the spirit of oppression.

The disobedience that is produced through oppressive unbelief points a condemning finger at others in an attempt to cover up the sins of the one committing them. In Genesis 3, we read how the snake in his cunning way convinced Eve—who then convinced Adam—to partake of the forbidden fruit. Upon eating the fruit, they both noticed that they were naked. So when God came through the garden and called for Adam, they both ran for cover.

Disobedience Will Lead You to the Wrong Place

When examining the reason why God called out for Adam, we learn that disobedience causes you to be out of your proper place. God would have normally just walked up and spoken to Adam, but on this day, Adam was out of place. You see, when you're out of God's will, you will ultimately run for cover.

Adam, who was originally empowered and created in God's exact image, was now oppressed and hiding from the One he so honorably conferred with every day.

> *And they heard the sound of the Lord God walking in the garden in the cool of the day, and Adam and his wife hid themselves from the presence of the Lord God among the trees of the garden* (Genesis 3:8).

So God addressed Adam in his disobedience and asked him, "Who told you that you were naked?" Of course, God already knew that the answer to this question was Satan. Adam, in his disobedience, had immediately entered into demonic fellowship by allowing the voice of Satan to override God's specific instructions. When one walks in disobedience, the voice of Satan is allowed to reign in his spiritual ear. And this can then "turn" him away from the things of God.

The oppressive voice of Lucifer is always speaking to capture, imprison, and oppress any who will listen —cunningly drawing them away from God and the blessings He ordained for their lives. If you have listened—whatever the fruit—and been caught in the chains of Satan's bondage, you need to know that this bondage can be broken through simple obedience to God's Word.

For Those Who Would Be Free

The first step to obtaining deliverance and victory is to make the decision to stop pointing a condemning finger at others and start admitting your own faults. You must not allow outside influences to take your focus off of God's divine direction for your life. Finger pointing only causes cover up and keeps one from repentance and re-entering full fellowship with God.

When God rebuked Adam in Genesis 3, Adam immediately pointed his finger at both God and Eve when he said:

> *"The woman whom You gave to be with me, she gave me of the tree, and I ate"* (Genesis 3:12).

Eve then pointed her finger at Lucifer:

> *And the Lord God said to the woman, "What is this you have done?" And the woman said, "The serpent deceived me, and I ate"* (Genesis 3:13).

In the end, it didn't matter who influenced who, or who sinned first, because all three had to pay the price for their disobedience. The serpent was made to crawl on his belly for eternity; the woman had to bear children in great pain and be dominated by the man;

and the man had to toil, working the ground to make provision for his family.

Disobedience changed Adam and Eve's lives forever in the garden. So those who say within themselves, "I'd rather sin now and repent later," must be willing to also say, "I'm willing to pay the price for my disobedience." Because sin has long-term effects, no one goes without warning from God before the cover is eventually snatched off of their sinful situation. Many use the scripture, *...His mercy endureth for ever...* (1 Chronicles 16:34), without realizing it was never intended to be used as a license for sin.

Oppression's Nagging Reminders of the Past

Once God covered Adam and Eve and forgave their sins, life moved on. But unbelief can be birthed out of fear and past disappointments. Abel's murder by Cain compelled Eve to ask God for a son to replace Abel. So Eve's third-born, Seth, was born. And when Seth matured, *to him also a son was born; and he named him Enosh. Then men began to call on the name of the Lord* (Genesis 4:26).

But it wasn't long before God had to condemn the whole world because of mankind's unbelief, destroying all except Noah and his family with a great flood. Why? Because Adam and Eve broke the trust factor, and Satan was there to remind every man of their own mistakes and tendencies to sin.

> *Then the Lord saw that the wickedness of man was great in the earth, and that every intent of the thoughts of his heart was only evil continually. And the Lord was sorry that He*

> *had made man on the earth, and He was grieved in His heart* (Genesis 6:5,6).

Many have experienced numerous disappointments in life. It is within this disappointing stage that a person can build a wall of distrust. Behind this wall often lies a lack of vision and initiative to strive for spiritual growth. Not only does the individual who hides behind this wall lack belief in God, but he also lacks trust in those around him. And taken to its furthest extreme, this kind of distrust can breed malice and hatred.

These types of individuals are also very prone to eventually giving up on life. They are afraid to step out in faith for fear of "getting their hopes up" only to face disappointment again.

People who are oppressed in a life of seemingly inescapable poverty, embarrassment, and disappointment, often choose to remain behind their wall for fear of continued failure. Satan's spirit of oppression ensures that the memory of their last failure or disappointment replays as a constant reminder of the agony they refuse to relive.

So within the oppressed may lie the desire to trust God and help others who are hurting, but they feel trapped behind this shield of "bad memories." And this vicious cycle births even more unbelief—which leads to more disobedience. This was the cycle that brought the earth to its utter destruction in Genesis 8.

Anyone who has been trapped behind one of these demonic barriers must invoke the power of God in his or her life if they are to be set free. The Word of God says, *My grace is sufficient for you, for My strength is made perfect in weakness"* (2 Corinthians 12:9). That means when you are too weak to fight for yourself, Jesus will make intercession for you, but, again, you must want to be set free. It's as simple as whispering a prayer in faith. Faith will break the curse of unbelief, releasing the ties that bind one in disobedience. Begin with repentance to God, not an apology.

True repentance comes from the heart with an honest effort on our part to abide in God's Word. Deliverance in some areas may be a gradual process. But steadfastness combined with faith, prayer, and fellowship with the Father, will allow you to ultimately walk in the liberating power of Christ.

If you need help in breaking through the barrier of oppressive disobedience and unbelief, pray the following prayer.

Father God, I come to You now, admitting that I've had some problems in the areas of unbelief and disobedience. But I'm sorry for falling into this oppressive trap of the devil, and I want Your forgiveness. Please help me to live an overcoming life in this area and to draw ever closer to You, for I realize that You are my strength. These things I ask in the precious name of Jesus. Amen.

8

MINISTERING TO THE OPPRESSED

Deliverance and Belief

But if the Spirit of Him who raised Jesus from the dead dwells in you, He who raised Christ from the dead will also give life to your mortal bodies through His Spirit who dwells in you (Romans 8:11).

As stated by the apostle Paul in the above scripture, if the Spirit of God resides within you, you can have life here on earth *through His Spirit who dwells in you.* Salvation through the blood of Jesus Christ promises a life free from oppression with liberty ruling and reigning throughout one's life. Just as your natural body grows and takes on new form as it is fed, so it is in the spirit. But there must be a willing, receptive heart.

When the Lord brought freedom to the Israelites in the Book of Exodus, many were still tempted to return to their spiritual and physical oppressor, Pharaoh. Why? Because many times when a person has been oppressed for so long, they tend to show more loyalty to their oppressor than they do to the one God has sent to free them.

For years the Israelites prayed unto God to set them free from their bondage in Egypt. Finally God heard their cry and sent His servant Moses.

> *"Now therefore, behold, the cry of the children of Israel has come to Me, and I have also seen the oppression with which the Egyptians oppress them"* (Exodus 3:9).

God instructed Moses on exactly what he was to say to both Pharaoh and to the Israelites. God knew these people had to know that Moses was sent by Him. When people are mistreated and misguided, they soon learn to trust no one. So sometimes they must be persuaded to be loosed, even though they've prayed for freedom and relief.

This was the case with the Israelites. They had prayed for many years for their freedom to worship God in liberty. But when freedom finally came, some still questioned whether or not their freedom was actually a curse. Many demanded their return to servitude under Pharaoh's harsh rule because the spirit of oppression never gives up. Even after God gave them direction and comfort with the physical manifestations of the plagues, pillar, and cloud, when turmoil arose, they turned on Moses.

So be advised, the one who is in bondage to Satan's oppression can be set free. But if you are ever sent as a deliverer, as I have been on many occasions, listen to God's Spirit, and never compromise.

When the altars are opened and the people respond (like the woman drawn into witchcraft spoken of in chapter 6 of this book), deliverance, though challenged, will manifest in Jesus' name. But when a spirit of unbelief infects those attending, that's another story. Let me tell you one.

A Deliverance Message Thwarted

Some time ago I was invited to preach at a church in another town that wasn't far from the town where my church was located. I was a guest speaker at an open-air tent meeting and agreed to speak for three nights.

The first night I ministered on *The Power of Protection* and taught on the role of angels in the lives of mortal men. This message was received wholeheartedly by the congregation and church leadership.

Then, the second night, the Lord directed me to minister on bondage. This message, which dealt with sexual bondage, rage, bad attitudes and behavior, was also joyously received by the congregation and the leaders of the church. In fact, the people cried out from the pews, echoing their relief that someone had finally arrived in their midst who would confront these issues.

But the pastor of the church was absent on this particular night, and one of the members telephoned the pastor to express their displeasure with the service. The pastor listened to this demon that controlled him through this member, and he became infuriated.

As a result, the pastor felt the need to deliver the congregation of my delivering message. This need to deliver had no bearing. It was an illusion that had been planted in the pastor's mind to snatch the Word that had been delivered and used to set the captives free.

A portion of my message had been taken from 1 Corinthians 6:9,10:

> *Do you not know that the unrighteous will not inherit the kingdom of God? Do not be deceived. Neither fornicators, nor idolaters, nor adulterers, nor homosexuals, nor sodomites, nor thieves, nor covetous, nor drunkards, nor revilers, nor extortioners will inherit the kingdom of God.*

You see, at the time (unbeknownst to me), this message had really hit home. There were people in this church who had been engaging in perversion. Homosexuality and lesbian relationships had been running rampant in this group, and the demons that possessed and controlled them were very angry.

The Fight Against Spiritual Freedom

Possessing spirits will go to any lengths to keep a person in bondage. So never underestimate their power or influence when engaging in spiritual warfare. This was the case in this church. The Word of God went forth with power, uncovering things that only the Spirit of God could have known, for I knew none of these individuals personally. The people cried out with loud voices as the message went forth. There were physical manifestations of deliverance and confessions from individuals who were participating in these acts of perversion. They wanted to be free.

You can always tell the spirits that have the strongest hold not only on an individual but within a church, because they cry out the loudest. The message I preached dealt with attitudes, adultery, fornication, jealousy, competition and sabotage—none of which received ANY negative response. But when I touched on homosexuality and lesbianism, there was a massive volcanic eruption, with loud cries of protest.

So the fight was on as these demonic forces moved in to secure their territory and re-inhabit the vessels who had been set free. So serious were these demons, that they used the most authoritative voice within the church—the pastor—to denounce the teaching of God's Word.

Moments before I was to preach the next night, the pastor felt it was necessary to soothe those who were offended by God's message on perversion. As I entered the tent—which was half full of my own church members—the pastor was busy tearing away at the message I'd preached the previous night.

Then I was faced with a major dilemma. Spiritual freedom comes from spiritual leaders. Romans 10:14 says: *And how shall they hear without a preacher?* So if you've been taught certain principles by someone you have great faith in, you will conform to what he or she teaches. "Like priest, like people."

You should always respect the leader God has placed in your life, yet never to the point of allowing what the leader says to override and belittle the Word of God.

So as I listened in amazement, I thought, *Do I go into another pastor's pulpit and challenge their leadership and authority? Do I challenge from their pulpit their teaching that neutralizes the Word of God? Or do I leave, allowing Satan to win this round of the battle?*

My decision was a swift one. I left and took my entire congregation with me. The Word of God was on my side, but the Bible says, *"Do not give what is holy to the dogs; nor cast your pearls before swine"* (Matthew

7:6). And in order to be fully delivered, a person must participate in his deliverance. I decided that my refutation of this pastor's refutation would only have produced a herd of angry pigs. Second Timothy 2:21 says there must be faithful participation in God's offer of deliverance:

> *Therefore if anyone cleanses himself from the latter, he will be a vessel for honor, sanctified and useful for the Master, prepared for every good work.*

So, I chose to move on.

The sad reality of the matter to me was, many of those people were waiting for deliverance, and I brought their liberating word. But as they took two steps in the direction of freedom, their spiritual leader told them, "There's no need to change. You're 'okay' the way you are because God loves you and He knows your heart." And those words closed the spiritual doors of bondage on the lives of many who were so jubilant the night before.

The spirit of a man gives forth life that must be protected and guarded from Satan's oppressing impurities. And the Word of God is what feeds the spirit, causing it to grow. This is why it is essential for a person to be planted in the right church, with a shepherd who speaks the Word of God with boldness and precision.

> *How shall they believe in Him of whom they have not heard? And how shall they hear without a preacher? And how shall they preach unless they are sent?* (Romans 10:14,15).

If God said it, it shall come to pass. But it's up to those who are captive to walk in His way of escape.

They must humble themselves in obedience to the Word of God in order to follow the leadership of the person God is using to bring freedom and liberty.

I pray this book has brought you new revelation about oppression...and its remedy. If you, or someone you know has been struggling with oppression, let the words on these pages bring the faith that is needed for total freedom. I trust you now understand that no matter how long an individual has been held captive to the spirit of oppression, he or she can be set free. The power is in God's Word and in the authority of Jesus' name.

So draw near unto God, and He will draw near unto you. And when He does, oppression's chains will break free.

> *Then Jesus said to those Jews who believed Him, "If you continue in My word, you are My disciples indeed. And you shall know the truth, and the truth shall make you free"* (John 8:31,32).

G.G. BLOOMER MINISTRY PRODUCTS

BOOKS

I'm Not Who You've Heard I Am	$5.95
Oppressionless	8.99
When Loving You Is Wrong But I Want To Be Right	11.99
Witchcraft In the Pews Who's Sitting Next to You	10.99
101 Questions Women Ask About Relationships	7.99

AUDIO CASSETTES

Shaking the Poison Loose	$5.00
Demons & How They Operate	5.00
The Witch Is Dead	5.00
Something Big	5.00
Foolish People	5.00
Jesus Sees You From Where He Is	5.00
Preparation Precedes Blessing	5.00
I'm Not Who I Told You I Was	7.00
It's the Law	7.00
NOW How Are You Going To Get Home?	7.00
The Tomb Is Empty	7.00
Be Eagle Minded	7.00
Saved, Being Saved, Going To Be Saved	7.00
If It Hasn't Come, It Will Come	7.00
Mr. Goodbar	7.00
God's Purpose For Time	7.00

You've Got What It Takes To Be Delivered 7.00
Noise, Bones, Breath, Shaking & Spirit. 7.00
Apples & Oranges (2-part series) 15.00
Breaking Generational Curses (2-part series) . 15.00
Breaking the Spirit of Poverty (2-part series) . 15.00
Engaged in Spiritual Warfare (3-part series) . . 15.00
God's Been Good To Us (2-part series) 15.00
It's Mess That Makes You (2-part series). 15.00
Preparation Precedes Blessing (3-part series) . 15.00
You Can Never Outgive God (2-part series) . . 15.00
KNOW Your Place (4-part series) 20.00
Witchcraft In the Pews (3-part series). 20.00

VIDEOS

Anointed Trio. $15.00
Be Eagle Minded 15.00
Breaking Generational Curses 15.00
But Elijah Is At the Gate. 15.00
God's Purpose For Time 15.00
I'm Not Who I Told You I Was. 20.00
It's Mess That Makes You. 20.00
Man In The Mirror 20.00
NOW How Are You Going To Get Home 20.00
Take the Keys and Unlock the Door 15.00
The Tomb Is Empty 20.00
Warning, Angels In Charge. 20.00
What Seal Is On Your Relationship? 15.00
Witchcraft In the Pews. 25.00

G.G. BLOOMER MINISTRIES
ORDER FORM

Title	(Please check one)	Unit Price	Qty.	Total
______________	☐ Book ☐ Tape ☐ Video	______		
______________	☐ Book ☐ Tape ☐ Video	______		
______________	☐ Book ☐ Tape ☐ Video	______		
______________	☐ Book ☐ Tape ☐ Video	______		
______________	☐ Book ☐ Tape ☐ Video	______		
______________	☐ Book ☐ Tape ☐ Video	______		
______________	☐ Book ☐ Tape ☐ Video	______		

TOTAL BEFORE SHIPPING ______

SHIPPING & HANDLING 2.00

TOTAL ENCLOSED ______
(including Shipping & Handling)

SHIP TO:

Name ______________________________

Address ______________________________

City ______________ State ____ Zip ______

Phone (____) ______________

Make checks payable to: G. G. Bloomer Ministries

MAIL TO: G. G. BLOOMER MINISTRIES
P.O. BOX 11563
DURHAM, NC 27703

Please allow 2-4 weeks for delivery. THANK YOU!